The Teen Witches' Guide to

Spells & Charms

Written by Claire Philip

Illustrated by Luna Valentine

ARCTURUS

SAFETY WARNING

This book features activities that involve the use of candles, paper, lighters, matches, herbs, oils, resins, and other similar materials. Always consult an adult before working with any of these items. Never light candles on or near anything that can catch fire. Never leave a candle burning unattended. Keep candles away from small children and animals.

The ideas, suggestions, and activities in this book are not intended to be a substitute for conventional medical advice. Always consult your doctor or other qualified healthcare professional before undertaking any alternative therapy to ensure that there are no contraindications for your health.

ARCTURUS

This edition published in 2023 by Arcturus Publishing Limited
26/27 Bickels Yard, 151–153 Bermondsey Street,
London SE1 3HA

Text adapted from *The Great Book of Spells* by Pamela Ball.

Author: Claire Philip
Illustrator: Luna Valentine
Designer: Rosie Bellwood
Editors: Donna Gregory and Rebecca Razo
Editorial Manager: Joe Harris
Indexer: Lisa Footitt

ISBN: 978-1-3988-2568-0
CH010877NT
Supplier 29, Date 0123, PI 00002507

Printed in China

Contents

This icon indicates the use of candles, lighters, and matches. Have an adult supervise you when working with these materials, and use caution.

Introducing Magic

What Are Spells?

Spells are a way of drawing on the strength of the unseen forces that exist within the Universe, using a combination of words and actions, as well as the power of your mind.

WHAT DO YOU NEED TO CAST A SPELL?

- The right spell or charm for your intention or goal
- Certain materials and supplies
- The correct timing
- A focused, peaceful state of mind
- The powers of the Universe!

DO NO HARM

Whenever you set out to create magic, always make sure that your intentions are pure and that you are seeking the highest good for yourself and anyone else involved. Never cast a spell for selfish reasons. Instead, engage with spells to discover the magic of our Universe and your inner creative power!

TYPES OF SPELLS

Invocations are spells that call on an unseen source of power, which differs from spell to spell.

Incantations are often very beautiful or rhythmic. Chanting, prayer, and hymns are, in many ways, incantations, especially when spoken with passion.

Love Spells aim to make someone attracted to another person. They should always be used with caution.

Bidding Spells are when a spell maker commands a particular thing to happen, without the cooperation of those involved.

Blessings might be counted as either prayers or spells— or as a kind of positive energy being sourced from beyond the spell maker toward a specific purpose.

Healing Spells are used to remind a person's body of its own ability to heal itself.

What Are Charms?

Technically, charms are any magical words, phrases, chants, and incantations spoken with the intention of protection; however, today they are mostly seen as objects that have been charged with magical energy.

Charms can also be objects that have symbolic meaning, such as a horseshoe or a four-leaf clover, and represent good luck.

Corn dollies are examples of enchanted poppets, or dolls, used in representational magic as charms for prosperity (see page 84).

SPOKEN CHARMS

Spoken charms are extremely powerful, particularly when their significance is known to some and not to others. The word "abracadabra" is an example of this. Today, it is seen as a joke word, but originally it was a chanted vibration designed to open doors that had been closed with magic!

Charms that involved actions, such as turning around clockwise three times, were often used in farming communities to protect against a bad harvest.

Setting up for Magic

Sacred Spaces

This chapter helps you get ready for spell-casting and charm-making. If you plan to cast a lot of spells or make many charms, you will probably want to set up a sacred space or altar. It doesn't matter if it is inside or outside—it just needs to be somewhere quiet where you can safely burn candles.

A sacred space needs to be dedicated to the purpose of working magic. You can do this by brushing the area clean and concentrating your thoughts on cleansing the space. Sprinkle the area with water and sea salt, and burn incense—such as frankincense—to clear it even more.

CREATING AN ALTAR

To turn a small table or surface (such as a tray or shelf) into an altar, you will need:

- Two candles with candleholders
- An incense holder and incense
- A small vase for fresh flowers or herbs
- Images or items that represent the energies you wish to work with—for example, a crystal to represent the element of Earth.

Before you add any items to your altar, cleanse them by washing them in salt water or by leaving them in direct sunlight or moonlight for a few hours. Before you place them on your altar, allow your energy—and energy from the Universe—to flow into the items.

Casting a Circle

A magic circle is an area in which you perform a spell. It is formed by your power, and it shuts out all distractions and negative energies. Before you cast a circle, purify your energy by meditating or taking a ritual bath.

 # METHOD:

- Ideally, wear something special that you only wear during spell-casting.
- Decide how big your circle will be; then purify that area by sprinkling it with water followed by salt. Your altar should stand in the middle of the circle.
- Meditate inside the circle for at least ten minutes—longer if possible.
- Imagine a circle of white light surrounding you and filling the circle.
- Circle the light around, above, and below you in a clockwise direction—feel it as a sphere around you.
- Say out loud that you banish any negative energy from the area.

- If you want to, place objects on the ground to show the boundaries of your circle; these can be candles, crystals, stones, flowers, or incense.
- Cast your spell, or make your charm from inside the circle!

Getting Yourself Ready

To cast a successful spell, you need to be calm, clear, and focused. The following activities can help you purify and balance your energy.

CLEANSING BATHS

This type of bath focuses on clearing your mind and body. All you need to do is place some Epsom salts into the water and set your intention. This clears your energy and makes you ready for spell-casting. You can light white candles (if it is safe to do so), or place a few drops of your preferred essential oil into the water. Remember that essential oils should never be used directly on the skin or ingested. Relax in the water for 10–20 minutes.

MEDITATION

A good meditation will put you in a relaxed state of mind, which is exactly what you need to cast a successful spell. Here is a very simple technique:

Sit or lie down somewhere comfortable. Close your eyes, if you wish, and slowly go through your five senses one by one. What can you taste? What can you feel? What can you see? What can you hear? What can you smell? Once you are aware of these sensations, be aware of all your senses at once; then let everything else flow away.

GROUNDING

Grounding yourself means balancing your physical, emotional, and mental energies by connecting to the Earth. Someone who is well-grounded lives in the present and feels both calm and secure. One way to ground yourself is to sit in a chair and place both feet on the ground. Imagine roots coming out from your feet and growing downward. Visualize yourself connecting to the Earth, and feel how supported and safe you are in this moment. Take this energy into your spell-casting.

Make a Simple Robe

Wearing special robes can also help get you in the right frame of mind for spell-casting as you begin to associate them with making magic. Some people like to wear a simple white robe, while others like to wear lots of different shades.

If you don't want to wear a robe, that is fine! As always, use your intuition to decide what is best for you.

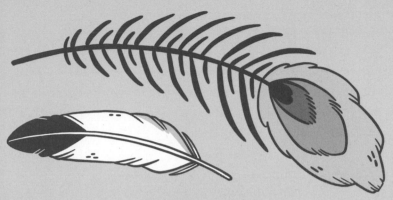

YOU WILL NEED:

- A piece of material that is at least twice your height. Its width needs to be at least the distance between your elbows when your arms are outstretched.
- Needle and thread
- Fabric paints and paintbrushes (optional)

METHOD:

- Fold the material over widthwise, and cut out a V-shaped piece from the middle of the folded side. This is for your head and neck.
- Sew up the two open sides leaving a hole for each of your arms.
- Turn the robe right side out so that the newly sewn seams are on the inside.
- If you like, embroider the front with a meaningful symbol, or use fabric paints to decorate your robe.

Making Incense

Making your own incense takes time, but it can be incredibly rewarding. Here's how to get started.

YOU WILL NEED:

- A set of measuring spoons
- A large mixing bowl
- Small containers with lids
- Labels
- Your chosen herbs, resins, oils
- Charcoal discs or blocks for burning the incense
- Mortar and pestle

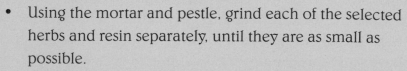

METHOD:

- Using the mortar and pestle, grind each of the selected herbs and resin separately, until they are as small as possible.
- When each ingredient is ground, add it to your mixing bowl (keep a small amount of each to one side so you can do a test run).
- Combine each ingredient well as you add it to the bowl. Add the oil last, mixing it in thoroughly.

- As you add each ingredient, you could say:"Make this herb [or resin, or oil] enhance the power of this offering."
- When all the ingredients are combined, spend some time thinking about what you want to use the incense for; then remix the incense.
- Ask for a blessing for the incense: "May this work of my two hands be blessed for the purpose of …"
- Test your sample by carefully lighting a charcoal disc and burning it on a heatproof surface.
- Fill the containers with your incense, label them clearly, and secure them tightly. Store them somewhere cool and dark.
- Your incense is now ready for use!

Here are some simple incense mixtures you can try:

FOR HEALING

- 2 parts myrrh resin
- 1 part cinnamon
- 1 pinch saffron

HOME BLESSING

- 1 part lavender
- 1 part basil
- 1 part hyssop
- Few drops of cucumber or melon oil

Choosing the Right Time

Over time, spell workers have discovered that taking action at certain times creates specific results. Each day of the week has a unique energy and power.

Use the "qualities" column on the table to look for the day of the week that best fits your spell's intention. You could choose items or images that represent the planet on your altar and use the corresponding hues, too.

DAY	PLANET	HUES	QUALITIES
Sunday	The Sun	Yellow, gold, orange	Advancement, ambition, authority figures, buying, career, children, drama, fun, goals, health, personal finances, success
Monday	The Moon	White, silver, grey, pearl	Antiques, archetypes, astrology, children, dreams, emotions, home, imagination, magic, psychology, short trips, water, women
Tuesday	Mars	Red, pink, orange	Action, aggression, beginnings, business, confrontation, gardening, movement, partnerships, passion, physical energy, sports

DAY	PLANET	HUES	QUALITIES
Wednesday	Mercury	Purple, magenta, silver	Accounts, advertising, astrology, communication, community, computers, contracts, education, healing, intelligence, languages, learning, legal matters, memory, music, siblings, wisdom, writing
Thursday	Jupiter	Blue, metallics	Broadcasting, business, charity, college, doctors, education, expansion, growth, logic, long-distance travel, luck, philosophy, political power, reading, researching, self-improvement, wealth
Friday	Venus	Green, pink, white	Affection, artists, beauticians, cosmetics, dancers, dating, decorating, designers, entertainers, fashion, friendships, gardening, gifts, harmony, income, luxury, marriage, poetry, relationships, romance, shopping, social activity
Saturday	Saturn	Black, grey, red, white	Binding, bones, criminals, death, debt, dentists, discovery, financing, hard work, justice, manifestation, obstacles, protection, structure, teeth, tests, transformation

You will also need to look at the best Moon phase since each stage has specific qualities, too (see next page).

23

The Moon Phases

Choosing the correct phase of the Moon is a vital element for many spells.

New Moon

The New Moon is a time for going deep within and reconnecting with your spiritual side.

First Quarter Moon

This is a time for initiating or planning a project or giving clarity.

Last Quarter Moon

This phase is a period to consider your achievements, taking the time to make the most of your experiences, as well as mourning any losses so that you can let them go.

Full Moon

This is a time for going out into the world, connecting with other people and expressing yourself creatively!

CONNECT TO THE MOON

This ritual can be performed indoors or outdoors and is designed to bring the energy of the Moon within your grasp until the next Full Moon. This very simple spell is an incantation.

YOU WILL NEED:

- A bowl of water
- White paper moon or flower (to represent the Moon)

METHOD:

- Raise the bowl toward the Full Moon in the sky and say:

HAIL TO THEE, WHITE SWAN ON THE RIVER. PRESENT LIFE, TIDE TURNER, MOVING THROUGH THE STREAMS OF LIFE. ALL HAIL MOTHER OF OLD AND NEW DAYS. TO YOU, THROUGH YOU, THIS NIGHT WE CLING TO YOUR AURA. PURE REFLECTION, TOTAL IN BELIEF, TOUCHED BY YOUR PRESENCE, I AM IN YOUR POWER AND WISDOM. PRAISE YOUR POWER, YOUR PEACE, MY POWER, MY PEACE. I AM STRONG. I PRAISE. I BLESS.

- Place your bowl down or on your altar, and stand for a few moments fully appreciating the power and beauty of the Moon.

Keeping Records

It is traditional for magic workers to record their spells for future reference. You will need to find an easy way of remembering what you have done. You can use the headings below to help you to do this.

SPELLS RECORD SHEET

Type of Spell

This should very clearly state what type of spell you are casting, whether it's a blessing, binding, love spell, etc.

Date and Time

Note the phase of the Moon, time of year, day of the week, and even hour of the day to begin tracking what works.

Reference

Find your own way of tracking your spells, perhaps by alphabet or theme, so that you can find them again easily.

Purpose

You should always state the purpose of your spell very clearly. This helps you focus your mind and ensures there is no doubt about your intention.

List of Ingredients or Supplies Needed

This will help if you need to replicate a spell—even one small difference can have a big effect.

Location

Some spells will be performed in specific places. By tracking locations, you may also spot places where your magic works best.

Results

Record all aspects of your results—anything that you feel is associated with your work. This record should include how successful you consider the spell to be and how it might be improved.

Elements or Deities

Always keep a note of any energies that you worked with.

Step-by-Step Instructions

Keep notes on your preparation stage as well as the spell itself. Often when spell-working, movements and words are intuitive and instinctive. The more you can remember, the more likely it is that you can recreate the same results again.

Additional Notes

There should be an area for you to write down anything noteworthy, so that you know what to expect next time.

THIS NEXT SECTION INTRODUCES SOME OF THE MAIN TYPES OF MAGIC AND GIVES EXAMPLES OF DIFFERENT SPELLS THAT FALL UNDER EACH CATEGORY. YOU'LL NOTICE THAT LOTS OF THEM OVERLAP!

Types of Magic & Spells

Candle Magic

CHOOSING OILS FOR CANDLE MAGIC

The following oils can be used to dress candles to perform quick, powerful spells. To complete a spell, the candle must burn all the way down, so you may wish to use a small candle or a tea light.

Always use a brand-new candle for each spell. If you don't, the effectiveness of your spell will be affected.

OIL	USE
Anise	Peaceful sleep
Bergamot	Money, success
Cinnamon	Attraction, speed, enhancing
Coconut	Purification, peace, intuition
Frankincense	Purification, luck
Frankincense and myrrh	Protection, purification, spirituality
Honeysuckle	Money, psychic powers

OIL	USE
Jasmine	Spiritual love
Lavender	Healing, peace, love
Lotus	Protection, healing, spirituality
Patchouli	Love, money
Peppermint	Healing, luck
Rose	Love, healing, beauty
Sage	Wisdom, purification, clarity
Sandalwood	Protection, purification, spirituality
Vanilla	Love, relationships
Ylang-Ylang	Opportunity, peace, spiritual balance

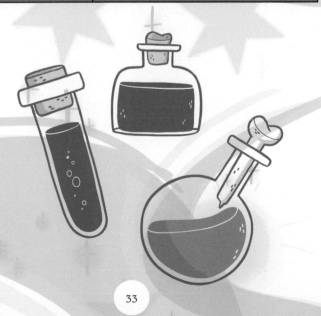

This kind of magic is simple. All you need is an intention, along with a candle and something to light it with!

HOW TO DRESS CANDLES

Before you start using candle magic, you need to "dress" the candle. Dressing a candle infuses it with the required vibration or energy for a spell. It also establishes a link between you and the candle.

YOU WILL NEED:

- A candle
- Your chosen oil
- A lighter

METHOD:

- Sit quietly and think about the intention (goal) of your spell.
- To bring something to you, rub the oil on the candle from the top of the candle to the middle, and then from the bottom to the middle.
- To send something away from you, rub the oil from the middle of the candle out to the ends.
- Say the following words (or something similar):

I CLEANSE AND CONSECRATE THIS CANDLE. MAY IT BURN WITH STRENGTH IN SERVICE OF THE GREATER GOOD.

A Spell to Gain Insight
into a Problem

This simple spell uses candle magic to help increase your intuition (your inner knowing). This one doesn't require oil.

YOU WILL NEED:

- A handful of uncooked barley
- A star anise pod
- A purple candle
- A pin
- A lighter

METHOD:

- Sit quietly and outline your problem to the Universe.
- Focus on your third eye (between your eyebrows in the middle of your forehead).
- Use the pin to inscribe some words about the situation onto the candle.
- Surround the candle with a circle of uncooked barley, and light it.
- Place the star anise pod inside the circle of barley.
- When the candle has burned, place the star anise pod under your pillow to gain insight into the issue through your dreams.

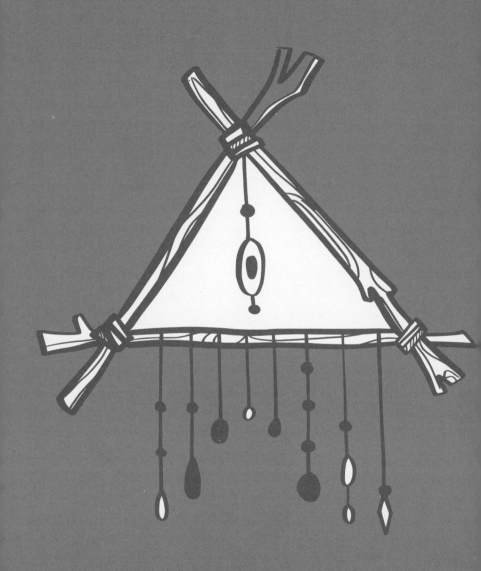

HUE MEANINGS

Different shades and tones can be used in your clothing, to dress your altar, or in your candles to represent the vibration you wish to introduce.

Black is the absence of light. It can be used to banish negativity.

Brown promotes the healing of the Earth. It symbolizes the home and relates to the animal kingdom. It can be used to blend several intentions.

Gold and Yellow represent vitality, strength, and rejuvenation. They are used to promote physical healing, hope, and happiness. These tones are related to the Sun and to the element of air, and they may be used for protection.

Green promotes love, fertility, beauty, prosperity, and wealth. Associated with the Earth, it suggests emotional health and healing.

Orange has a healing vibration, particularly for relationships. It is associated with material success and legal matters. A highly creative vibration, it often relates to childhood and emotional stability.

Pink is often associated with friendship, love, and healing emotions. It also symbolizes creativity and innocence.

Purple, Indigo, and Violet are associated with royalty and importance. They are also associated with wisdom, vision, dignity, and fame. They command respect and promote both psychic and mental healing.

Red is associated with passion, intensity, fire, and courage.

Silver is almost always associated with the Moon.

Sky Blue signifies communication in all its forms, not just between people, but between Earth and the unseen realms. It is good for meditative practices and for help with studying and learning.

White symbolizes purity and spirituality; it contains the whole spectrum of visible light.

A Spell to Balance
Your Energies

This spell can be performed during the day or at night.

YOU WILL NEED:

- Green and yellow candles
- Fresh flowers for your sacred space or altar
- A single white flower
- A bowl of water large enough to hold the flower
- Jasmine or rose incense
- A lighter

METHOD:

- Prepare your sacred space as usual, being sure to use plenty of fresh flowers to decorate.
- Float the single white candle in the bowl of water while thinking of its beauty.
- Light the candles while thinking of the freshness of Mother Nature's energies.
- Light the incense, and become aware of all the intermingling scents being created.

- Quietly consider the power of nature.
- Stand with your feet hip-distance apart. Become aware of your connection to Earth, mentally reaching toward its core through the soles of your feet.
- Feel energy in the form of light rising through you.
- Feel the light swirling through you, cleansing, healing, and balancing your energy.
- When you feel refreshed, run your hands over your body from head to toe.
- Sit quietly for a while to let the energy settle in your body. Think about how you will use your new energy.

A Spell to Bring about Change

This candle magic spell can help you move forward into a new situation.

YOU WILL NEED:

- Two small white candles
- An oil that represents the old situation you are leaving behind
- An oil that represents the new situation you are moving toward—use your intuition to choose
- Two plain pieces of paper
- A pen and a lighter

METHOD:

- Dress the candle with your chosen oil and light it.
- On the paper, write down the things you are moving away from or wish to leave behind. Think carefully about each one.
- When the candle is three-quarters burned through, tear up the piece of paper into tiny shreds—to be rid of the old.

- Let the candle completely burn out.
- If there are elements of the old situation that you wish to take forward, light a new candle that you have dressed for the new situation.
- This time, write what you hope for from the new situation on a fresh piece of paper, and place it under the candle as you allow it to burn down.
- Keep this piece of paper safe—sleep with it under your pillow for three nights or until you feel you have truly taken on the new ideas!

A Spell to Remove Bad Luck

This spell is a lot like the previous one, but it is a little more complicated. It is best performed on the night of a Full Moon.

YOU WILL NEED:

- A candle to represent yourself in your astrological shade (see chart on opposite page)
- An orange candle for sudden change and success
- A silver or light grey candle for the neutralization of bad luck
- A dark candle to represent bad luck
- A magenta candle to speed up the luck-changing process
- Rosemary oil
- A lighter

METHOD:

- Dress all the candles, apart from the magenta one, with the oil. Remember: you are moving bad luck away from you.
- Dress the magenta candle to bring in what you desire.
- Put the candles in a place where they can burn safely.
- Light the candle that represents you and say: "This is me and everything that I am."
- Light the dark candle and say: "This is my bad luck. It must now leave me. May it be transformed now and henceforth."
- Light the grey candle and say: "This will counteract any

bad luck. It will dissolve into the void and become nothing."

- Light the orange candle and say: "This represents the good changes that are coming into my life. I welcome success with open arms."
- Light the magenta candle and say: "This is the energy to bring about the change."
- Sit for several minutes repeating: "I welcome change. I welcome the incoming good."
- Allow the candles to burn out completely.

ASTROLOGICAL SIGN	CANDLE SHADE
Aries	Red
Taurus	Green
Gemini	Yellow
Cancer	Pale Blue, Silver
Leo	Gold, Orange
Virgo	Rich Brown
Libra	Royal Blue, Pink
Scorpio	Dark Red
Sagittarius	Purple, Dark Blue
Capricorn	Dark Brown, Black
Aquarius	All
Pisces	Sea Green, Mauve

Herbal Magic

HERBAL USES

Many magical practices, including spell work and charms, make use of herbs. Their properties mean that they create a type of force field that intensifies the vibration of a spell or charm. Simply having herbs in your sacred space or having them around you can begin the process of enhancing the area or your personal vibration. Here are some common herbal uses:

Attraction
Juniper (dried berries worn as a charm), lemon, patchouli

Banishing
Lilac

Cleansing
Cinnamon, clove, pine

Courage
Basil, garlic, nettle, thyme

Friendship
Lemon, rose, passionflower

Good Fortune
Heather, nutmeg, rose

Happiness
Anise, marjoram, saffron

Harmony
Hyacinth, lilac, meadowsweet

Healing
Aloe, chamomile, cinnamon, eucalyptus, fennel, garlic, marjoram, mint, nettle, onion, pine, rosemary, saffron, sage, sandalwood, thyme, willow

Love
Apple, basil, coriander, dill, ginseng, honeysuckle, jasmine, lavender, lemon, lemon balm, marigold, marjoram, meadowsweet, rose, rosemary, vanilla

Luck
Apple, hazel, mint, rose

Meditation
Chamomile, frankincense

Mental Powers
Caraway, rosemary, vanilla, walnut

Money
Chamomile, cinnamon, cinquefoil, clove, fennel, ginger, mint

Peace
Aloe, chamomile, lavender, violet

Power
Carnation, cinnamon, ginger, rosemary

Prosperity
Acorn, almond, ash, basil, honeysuckle

Protection
Aloe, anise, basil, black pepper, caraway, chamomile, cinquefoil, clove, coriander, dill, fennel, fern, garlic, hawthorn, holly, lavender, lilac, marjoram, meadowsweet, nettle, onion, rose, rosemary, sage, sandalwood

Purification
Anise, cinquefoil, fennel, frankincense, lavender, lemon, pine, rosemary, sandalwood, thyme

Success
Cinnamon, ginger, lemon balm, lavender, thyme

Spirituality
Cinnamon, clover, frankincense, myrrh, sandalwood

Wisdom
Sage, sunflower

TYPES OF HERBAL SPELLS

PROTECTION SPELLS	Some herbs can be used to guard against injury and accidents.
LOVE	The vibration of certain herbs helps you meet new people, overcome shyness, or let others know that you are open to new relationships.
HEALING	Many herbs have healing properties that can help from both a magical and physical viewpoint.
LUCK	Luck is the knack of being in the right place at the right time and being able to act on instinct! Luck herbs help you create your own good fortune.
MONEY	Certain herbs create an environment in which money can come to you—even as a gift, a pay rise, or something else!
HEALTH	The smell and vibration of fresh herbs can help restore good health.

A Spell Bottle to Protect the Home

Spell bottles are a bringing together of energy. They are created and enhanced to achieve a specific magical goal. This spell uses the herb rosemary to protect the home.

YOU WILL NEED:

- A small glass jar with a tight-fitting lid
- Fresh rosemary
- Pins
- Needles
- Red fruit juice
- Red candle

METHOD:

- Flow your energy into the jar, while filling it with the rosemary, pins, and needles.
- While doing this, say these words to enhance the action:

NEEDLES, HERB, JUICE, AND PINS—
PROTECT NOW THIS HOUSE OF MINE.
IN THIS BOTTLE, I NOW TRUST—AS IN
THE GROUND, IT IS THRUST.

- Pour in the juice, and seal the jar with wax from the candle.
- Bury the bottle in or near your yard, garden, or as close to your front door as possible.
- Trace a protective pentagram over the bottle using your fingers; then leave it alone, knowing you are protected. As you move your fingers, imagine a bright purple light streaming down to form the shape.

If the movements of planet Venus, as seen from Earth, were plotted on a chart, the shape of a pentagram star would be revealed!

A Spell to Remove Fear

This spell uses herbs, visualization, and relaxation to deal with fear.

YOU WILL NEED:

- Herbs for courage such as basil, garlic, nettle, or thyme
- A red candle and a lighter

METHOD:

- Place the herbs on your altar.
- Place the candle in the middle of your altar, and light it.
- Say the following words three times:

HEAR ME, I CALL UPON COURAGE
TO RELINQUISH THE HOLDING TIES
OF FEAR. BREAK THEM,
LEAVE ME FAR AWAY,
LET THEM NOT BE NEAR.

- Breathe deeply for about 10–15 minutes, and concentrate on your fear fading away.
- Let the candle burn out completely.
- Gather the herbs and the candle, and bury everything in the ground as far away from your house as possible.

A Spell to Drive Away Bad Dreams

This spell uses herbal magic to clear your bedroom of any negative influences. Rosemary and sage are great herbs for this spell. It should be performed as the Moon wanes.

YOU WILL NEED:

- A bowl of warm water
- Salt
- A sprig of rosemary or sage
- String

METHOD:

- Dissolve the salt in the warm water.
- Tie the herbs together, and dip them in the water. Use them to sprinkle the water in the corners of your room.
- Use the sprig to sprinkle the water on your bedding, paying particular attention to the head and foot of the bed.
- Place the herbs under your pillow or under the middle of the bed.
- The next morning, discard the herbs at a crossroads or bury them as far away from your home as you can—this carries all negativity away from your bedroom and bed.

Crystal Magic

CHOOSING YOUR CRYSTALS

Crystals and gems have special qualities that can be used in magic. Even ordinary stones have their own power and can be used to store all sorts of energies and powers.

Use this method whenever you are about to buy a new crystal. It can help you find the specific stones for you.

- Stand in front of a group of crystals.
- Close your eyes; then open your eyes quickly. Focus on the first crystal that attracts you in any way.

- Pick it up and see how it feels in your hand. If your hand tingles or you have another physical reaction, it could be the one for you.
- Other times, you may be drawn to a crystal without knowing why. Trust your instincts!
- If you are selecting a crystal for a specific purpose, hold that purpose in your mind as you choose.

CLEANSING YOUR CRYSTALS

Whenever you get a new crystal, cleanse it and dedicate it to your intention. Here are some ways you can cleanse a crystal:

- Clean it in salt water or seawater; then leave it in sunlight or moonlight to energize.
- Pass it through the smoke of your preferred incense until it feels clear.
- Clean it in a flowing stream, visualizing the crystal becoming clear by the movement of the water.

To assign an intention to a crystal, place it in sunlight or moonlight at either the Full or New Moon. As you do so, state your intent.

CONNECTING WITH YOUR CRYSTALS

The following meditation techniques can help you connect with your crystals before you use them in charms or spells.

Before You Start

Find a quiet place and spend a few moments relaxing while holding your crystal. Become aware of the energy link between you and the crystal. Once that link has been established, you will be able to ask the crystal to deliver on a particular purpose.

TECHNIQUE ONE

Sit in a place where you won't be disturbed. Hold the crystal in your left hand. Close your eyes and breathe in slowly. Release the breath. Try to achieve a slow, regular rhythm of breathing. Eventually, you will reach a relaxed state where you do not need to concentrate. When this happens, on your in-breath imagine drawing in power. On your out-breath, send it to wherever it needs to go.

TECHNIQUE TWO

Place your crystal on a table or your altar. Sit or stand in front of it, and concentrate on the crystal. Allow your eyes to close naturally, maintaining the picture of the crystal in your mind. Remember the purpose of your meditation—to connect with the crystal— and focus on the idea that the crystal supports that purpose. You can do this many times to keep building your connection.

A LIST OF CRYSTALS

Amber Usually golden, this stone turns negative energy into positive energy and helps the body start to heal itself.

Agate A member of the quartz family, agate is a general healer. It is especially good for improving self-esteem.

Amethyst This type of quartz is usually a rich purple. It helps with creative thinking and is a protector against blood diseases, grief, and insomnia.

Aquamarine Good for the eyes, aquamarine helps with nerve, throat, liver, and stomach troubles.

Aventurine A quartz stone found in various shades—often green. It can help with some skin conditions.

Bloodstone A dark-green quartz flecked with red jasper; bloodstone strengthens the will to do good.

Carnelian A translucent red or orange stone; carnelian strengthens the voice and can be helpful for depression.

Chrysoprase This stone opens and activates the energy of the heart, and it encourages compassion and self-acceptance.

Citrine A form of quartz, citrine is yellow. Wearing this crystal may give you greater control over your emotions and help blood circulation. It is often associated with wealth.

Emerald This precious stone is a deep dark green. Emerald improves intellect and memory, and may help with insomnia.

Garnet A group of gemstones that range from a deep blood red to orange and purplish red. Garnet helps with self-confidence and self-esteem.

Gold This well-known metal is said to improve a person's character through learning. It also helps with responsibility and depression.

Jade This green stone may help with kidney issues.

Jasper This often red type of quartz can increase a person's sense of smell and can help with liver or kidney problems.

Kunzite This stone activates loving thoughts and communication. It can be used to remove negative energies and protect against them.

Lapis Lazuli A mixture of minerals, lapis lazuli is usually deep blue with flecks of fool's gold (also called pyrite). It is useful for heart conditions.

Malachite An attractive ornamental stone, malachite is a vivid green. The copper in malachite can help with asthma.

Moonstone This stone has a milky sheen and is often bluish. Moonstone fosters inspiration and enhances the emotions.

Obsidian Found in both red and black, obsidian is an excellent grounding stone.

Onyx Jet-black onyx aids concentration and can help with ear problems.

Peridot Bottle-green peridot has a soft and shiny appearance. It helps with digestion.

Rock Crystal A clear, pure quartz, rock crystal is an important healing stone that helps its wearer by improving intuitive powers.

Rose Quartz A translucent crystal, rose quartz sparks the imagination and calms the emotions. It is associated with love.

Ruby A precious stone, ruby improves mental ability.

Sapphire Usually blue, sapphire can also be clear, yellow, or green. This stone of friendship and love brings devotion, faith, and imagination.

Smoky Quartz This common crystal is used to give good luck.

Tiger's Eye This beautiful brown-gold stone is worn or used for clearer thinking.

Tourmaline Tourmaline attracts inspiration, goodwill, and friendship.

Turquoise A great protector, turquoise is a good stone to give as a present.

A Spell to Bless the Home

This blessing uses crystals, herbs, and candle magic to clear the energy of a house.

YOU WILL NEED:

- A handbell
- Salt water
- Rosemary herb or oil
- Light-blue candles
- Tea light candles and holders
- Large quartz crystal
- Several pieces of onyx or obsidian
- Two pieces of rose quartz
- A lighter

METHOD:

- Start in the kitchen—the heart of the home. Remain quiet for a few moments, and focus on the purpose of the blessing.
- Walk through each room of the house, ringing the bell and sprinkling the salt water—don't forget the corners! End your walk in the kitchen where you started.
- Repeat this process, this time holding lit candles and sprinkling rosemary. (Get an adult's permission first!)

- Repeat a blessing as you go. The words can be as simple as, "Bless this home from above; keep it safe and filled with love."
- Return to the kitchen and chant "Om." This sound is said to be the sound of the Universe and is pronounced—"Aum." Feel the sound swelling and imagine it filling the home. Place the large quartz crystal in this room, so it can become a power source for the other crystals.
- Walk around the house for a final time with your oil and stones. Place a piece of onyx or obsidian in each room.
- Place the rose quartz on either side of the main entrance to the house.
  - Draw a protective pentagram with your fingers (see page 53) over each opening into the house, including all doors, windows, fireplaces, and vents.

A Spell to Help Heal Others

This spell uses crystals, candles, and incense.

YOU WILL NEED:

- A clear quartz crystal
- Three candles—blue for healing, white for power, and pink for love
- Healing incense
- Paper with the name of the person you wish to be healed
- A lighter

METHOD:

- Place the candles on your altar in a semicircle, with the white candle in the middle.
- Light the incense.
- Place the paper with the person's name in the middle.

- Put the quartz on top of the paper.
- Be aware of your energy linking with whatever you consider to be the Divine.
- Breathe in the incense, and feel your energy increasing with each breath.
- When you feel ready, release the energy. Imagine it passing through the crystal to the recipient.
- As you do this, say the following: "[Person's Name] be healed by the gift of this Power."

A Spell to Bring Romantic
Love to You

YOU WILL NEED:

- A sprig of rosemary
- A piece of rose quartz
- Rose or vanilla incense
- A pink or red candle
- A small box
- Red pen
- A lighter

METHOD:

- Sit somewhere that feels particularly powerful to you. It could be at your altar, under a special tree, or by a running stream.
- Write in red on the box, "Love is mine."
- Light the incense, then place the rosemary and rose quartz inside the box along with anything else that represents love to you—this could be drawings of hearts, poems, anything!
- Imagine yourself happy and in love.
- Light the candle and say:

I AM LOVE,
LOVE I WILL FIND.
TRUE LOVE PREFERABLY
WILL SOON BE MINE.

LOVE IS ME,
LOVE I SEEK.
MY TRUE LOVE,
I WILL SOON MEET.

- Continue concentrating on being happy; then put out the candle and add it to the box.
- Let the incense burn out then seal the box. Don't open it until you've found love!
- When you have found your love, take out the rose quartz and keep it as a reminder.
- Bury the entire box in the ground.

Knot Magic

MAKE YOUR OWN MAGIC CORD

Although it isn't very well known, knot magic has been around since ancient times. It often involves tying and untying knots to either bind or release energies at certain times. This long braid can be used in many knot spells.

YOU WILL NEED:

- Three lengths of cord 2.7 m (9 ft) long in a shade that is significant to you.

METHOD:

- Start braiding the three cords together. As you do, think of three becoming one.
- Concentrate all your energy on what you are doing, imagining that the braid is an extension of you.
- Tie a knot on both ends to keep the braid together.
- Place it on your altar. With your dominant hand, make three counterclockwise circles above it while saying, "I hereby cleanse and purify you. I send away any defilement that may lie within."
- Visualize the cord surrounded by bright light.
- Imagine it shining brightly; then let the image fade away.
- Make three clockwise circles above the cord while saying, "I bless and consecrate you for the purpose of [state intention]."

- Once again, see the cord surrounded by bright light.
- Hold the image for as long as you can, and then let it fade.

  - When not in use, keep the braid protected by wrapping it in a clean cloth.

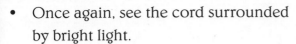

Knot magic works on the principle of binding and weaving—you can use ribbon, rope, string, yarn, or anything else that can be knotted or braided! It is a type of representational magic (see page 80).

Tying Knots

When you are ready to start casting knot spells, you can use this method to tie the knots in your cord. As you tie each knot, think about the outcome you want to achieve. As you tie the final (ninth) knot, allow your energy to direct itself into the cord and its knots. Do this by imagining the energy flowing out of you in the form of white light.

BY KNOT OF ONE, THE SPELL'S BEGUN.
BY KNOT OF TWO, IT COMETH TRUE.
BY KNOT OF THREE, SO IT SHALL BE.
BY KNOT OF FOUR, THIS POWER IS MORE.
BY KNOT OF FIVE, 'TWILL NOW SURVIVE.
BY KNOT OF SIX, THIS SPELL I FIX.
BY KNOT OF SEVEN, LET IT BE GIVEN.
BY KNOT OF EIGHT, NOW WELCOME FATE.
BY KNOT OF NINE, WHAT'S DONE IS MINE.

Knot magic is good for spells where you want something to happen slowly—you can use the knots to "trap" the energy and then use it. Just make sure that you remember which knot you tied first! You must untie them in the same order in which they were tied.

On the first day, untie the knot that was tied first. On the second day, move on to the second knot, and so on until all the knots are untied. Each day, just before you untie your knot, visualize the outcome you intend. As you release the knot, release the power!

Tying a Knot for Love

YOU WILL NEED:

- Three lengths of cord or string 2.7 m (9 ft) long in various pastel tones such as pink, red, and green.

METHOD:

- Braid the cords tightly together, while concentrating on what you want.
- Firmly tie a knot near one end of the braid, thinking of your desire.
- Tie another knot, and then another, until you have tied seven knots, equally spaced apart.
- Wear or carry the cord with you until you find your true love.
- Afterward, keep the cord somewhere safe, or burn it and scatter the ashes in a stream.

A Spell to Cure Sickness

This spell works on the principle that you can bind the illness into the cord.

YOU WILL NEED:

- 20 cm (8 in) length of cord
- A large jar
- Salt to fill half the jar
- Piece of paper and pen
- Rubber band

METHOD:

- Clear your energy and become fully grounded before you start.
- Mark the cord six times, so you have seven equal lengths.
- Repeat the words below six times. Tie a knot each time you speak:

SICKNESS, NO ONE BIDS YOU STAY;
IT'S TIME FOR YOU TO FADE AWAY.
THROUGH THESE KNOTS,
I BID YOU LEAVE; BY THESE WORDS
WHICH I DO WEAVE.

- Put the cord in the jar of salt.
- Create a lid for the jar with the words above written on a piece of paper. Put the rubber band around the top of the jar to hold it in place.
- Bury the jar or dispose of it appropriately.

Representational Magic

HOW TO MAKE A CLOTH POPPET

This type of magic involves utilizing an object that represents someone or something for which you are working the spell. Poppets, or dolls, are a great example of representational magic. They are small figurines made from wood, paper, material, or clay shaped roughly into human form. You should only ever make a poppet of someone else if they have given you permission, such as when you wish to help someone.

YOU WILL NEED:

- Paper or card
- Soft material, such as felt or cotton
- Needle and thread
- Scissors
- Straw, paper, or cotton wool
- Herbs associated with your intention (optional)

METHOD:

- Draw the outline of a simple human figure on the card or paper, and cut it out.
- Fold the material in two, and place the template on top. Carefully cut around it.
- Sew the figures together, leaving a small area open.
- Turn the figure right-side out, so that the stitches are now on the inside.
- Stuff the figure with straw, paper, cotton, or herbs; then finish sewing the material together.
- Draw on facial figures if you wish!

Your poppet is now ready for use! Do not destroy it when you are finished with it— either give it to the person it represents, or bury it safely in the ground.

Make a Healing Poppet

Make a cloth poppet using the instructions on page 84, but this time include within the poppet something that represents the person you are hoping to help.

For a solution to a short-term problem, you might include a lock of hair. For a solution to a long-term problem, you might include a crystal representing the person concerned—perhaps one that matches their astrological sign.

YOU WILL NEED:

- Poppet
- Blue candle
- Salt water

> In this spell, you create the poppet not to represent the problem that someone is having, but to create an image of the solution.

METHOD:

- Create your poppet to represent the person you wish to help—make sure it shows them as healed and whole.
- Take the doll into your sacred space. Light a blue candle to represent healing.
- Sprinkle the poppet with salt water and say:

THIS FIGURE I HOLD MADE BY MY ART
HERE REPRESENTS [PERSON'S NAME].
BY MY ART MADE,
BY MY ART CHANGED,
MAY NOW THEY BE HEALED,
BY ART DIVINE.

- Carefully pass the poppet above the flame of the candle, and visualize the person being cleansed of their problem.
- Hold the poppet in both hands, and breathe on it gently. Visualize the poppet and the person being filled with healing energy from the Divine. Pay particular attention to areas of the body they are having issues with.
- Focus the idea of mental healing onto the poppet.
- Finally, imagine spiritual energy infusing the doll—and therefore your friend—with the spiritual help that they need by visualizing them being filled with white light. See them as well, happy, and filled with energy.
- Keep the poppet in your sacred space until it is no longer needed. At this time, enter your sacred space, take the poppet, sprinkle it with water and say:

BY DIVINE ART CHANGED,
BY MY ART MADE,
FREE THIS POPPET FROM
THE CONNECTION WITH [PERSON'S NAME].
LET IT NOW BE UNMADE.

- If the poppet contains direct links with the person—such as hair—burn it in an open fire (ask an adult to help you). If it does not, dispose of it in any way you wish. If you have used a crystal, this should be cleansed by holding it under running water; then give it to the person as a keepsake or for protection.

AMULETS AND TALISMANS

Amulets and talismans are powerful representational magical objects used for protection and good luck. Amulets are most often worn, while talismans can be carried. The powers of a talisman come from cosmic forces beyond the object; whereas, amulets contain a power of their own.

Lots of natural objects can be used as amulets—for example, acorns, arrowheads, beads, cowrie shells, feathers, and even pine cones. These items are things that people often collect if they come across them—perhaps we can intuitively sense their power!

Ancient Egyptians placed great importance on amulets. The Eye of Horus ensured universal protection, ankhs represented everlasting life, and the scarab signified resurrection after death.

Moon Protection
for Amulets

This technique can be used to protect an object that you want to use as an amulet. It is best performed during a Full Moon.

YOU WILL NEED:

- Your chosen amulet
- A glass of spring water

METHOD:

- Place your amulet in the cup of spring water one day before the Full Moon.
- The following day, stir the water three times with the fingers on your right hand in a clockwise motion.
  - Take the cup in your hands and swirl the water around, moving the cup in a clockwise, circular, stirring motion three times.
  - Say these words aloud:

OH, LIGHT OF THE MOON,
WRAP ME,
PROTECT ME,
KEEP ME FROM HARM.

- Remove your amulet from the cup, and raise it up to the sky to acknowledge the Moon.
- Lower the cup, bring it to your lips; then place on your altar.
- Carry the amulet with you till the next Full Moon.

OBJECTS FOR USE AS AMULETS

Use likenesses in the form of charms or small sculptures of
the following symbols, natural objects, and animals
to harness and embody their power.

Acorn An acorn symbolizes new beginnings and
rebirth. To increase your wealth, place three
drops of pine oil onto an acorn during a
waxing moon, and bury it in your yard,
garden, or as close to the front door as
possible!

Anchor An anchor represents stability, hope, and salvation. It
represents all matters to do with the sea and
protects against physical harm.

Ankh Also called the Egyptian Cross of Life,
the ankh is the key to wisdom and hidden
mysteries. It represents creative energy, making
it a strongly protective symbol. It brings health
and abundance.

Ant An amulet in the form of an ant will help the wearer
be hard-working. Placed on an altar, it will attract career
opportunities!

Arrowhead Carry an arrowhead for protection against enemies, bad luck, jealousy, and all negative forces.

Bamboo Bamboo represents truth, integrity, and lasting friendship. It also symbolizes healthy old age.

Bat This creature signifies long life. It is especially beneficial to educational matters and is said to bring good fortune.

Bear The bear is the guardian of the world and symbolizes inner knowing and healing.

Beads These are magically significant whether they are made from crystal or ordinary materials. They are often worn as necklaces or pendants.

Bees The bee represents immortality and the soul. As an amulet, it brings wealth through inspiration and intuition.

Birds As amulets, birds protect the wearer on long journeys and ensure safe travels.

Butterfly This widely accepted symbol of the psyche and the soul signifies the continuous cycle of life, death, and resurrection. It suggests joy, laughter, and pleasure.

Castle Symbolizing self-knowledge, the castle is a strongly protective image. It suggests the doorway to knowledge and power.

Corn This representation of Mother Nature signifies abundance, fertility, and wealth.

Cowrie Shell This shell represents prosperity.

Crown The crown signifies justice and fair dealings.

Crocodile Wearing this symbol as an amulet is a protection against the negative.

Deer This embodies compassion and grace.

Dog Loyalty and guardianship are qualities inherent in the dog. Wearing this amulet signifies protection.

Dolphin Wise and happy, the dolphin suggests the exploration of deep emotion and psychic abilities.

Dragon The dragon by tradition symbolizes royalty and riches. It is a symbol of heaven, the Sun, and the essence of nature. It is also a protection against bad fortune.

Dragonfly This suggests imagination and breaks through illusions, thus gaining power and understanding through any dreams you may have.

Eagle The eagle signifies the expectation of power, high ideals, and good fortune.

Eye of Horus Also known as the "all-seeing eye," this is an ancient symbol used as an amulet for wisdom, prosperity, spiritual protection, and good health.

Flowers These are manifestations of developing life and nature; they represent spring and beauty.

Four-Leaf Clover Good fortune is said to smile on you if you carry a four-leaf clover. It is believed to be the most powerful of all-natural amulets.

Frog To promote friendship or reconcile enemies, engrave the image of a frog on a piece of beryl, and wear it as a necklace!

Garlic One of the oldest and most familiar natural protection amulets.

Gods and Goddesses An amulet or representation of any of the gods and goddesses immediately puts the wearer or carrier under their protection.

Hare The hare stands for regeneration, fertility, and rebirth.

Hawk The hawk signifies all-seeing perception and observation. A hawk amulet would be worn for protection and to give focus to your life.

Heart In ancient Egypt, the heart was said to represent the soul. More universally, it represents the seat of love and devotion.

Hippopotamus As an amulet, it wards off bad tempers and stands for regeneration.

Horse The image of a horse symbolizes freedom, stability, and courage.

Horseshoe The horseshoe is a well-known symbol of good luck in many parts of the world.

Jaguar Symbolizing spiritual wisdom and focused power, an amulet in this form protects and encourages.

Leaf Signifying growth, the symbol of the leaf means rejuvenation, hope, and a revival of energy.

Lion The lion symbolizes nobility and is a symbol of the Sun. It protects through courage, and as an amulet it represents the courage of conviction.

Lizard An amulet in the form of a lizard is said to give vision in farsightedness and the ability to create an acceptable future.

Lotus The lotus is a powerful symbol representing serenity and that which is manifested from purity.

Mouse The mouse represents innocence, faith, and trust. Worn as an amulet, it reminds the wearer of the necessity of keeping an eye for detail.

Mushroom The mushroom stands for hidden wisdom and mystic power.

Owl To increase knowledge, wear an amulet made of gold, silver, or copper. The symbol of the owl brings good luck.

Oyster Shell In Egypt, the oyster shell as an amulet meant "sound, whole, and healthy."

Peacock The peacock suggests long life and enduring love.

Phoenix The phoenix as a bird symbolizes transformation and regeneration. It represents the continuity of life and overcoming obstacles.

Pineapple A symbol of fertility, the pineapple represents good fortune and fruitfulness.

Pine Cone The pine cone, with its many seeds, signifies abundance, health, wealth, and power. Worn as an amulet or kept within the home, it is said that you will never lack the good things of life.

Pyramid Crystals shaped like pyramids possess the power to balance emotions and are said to bring wisdom. It is thought that wearing an amulet in the shape of a pyramid improves concentration and increases or re-energizes psychic powers.

Raven The raven represents inner journeys and dreams. It also represents mystery.

Rice Grains Grains of rice are representative of fertility and essential nourishment.

Rose The rose with four petals signifies femininity and earthly possessions.

Scarab Beetle One of the most famous of all Egyptian amulets, the sacred scarab is a symbol of the perpetual renewal of life. It stands for health and strength. Wear scarab beetle charm for good luck.

Seashells These are a symbol of femininity. Signifying birth and regeneration, they can be worn as charms, placed on altars, or kept on the person as a sign of allegiance.

Skull To help break the chains of any addiction, wear a gold skull-shaped charm necklace as a magical amulet.

Snake The snake has always stood for transformation because of its ability to shed its skin. As an amulet, it reminds us of the necessity for constant change and transformation.

Spider An amulet worn in this form reminds the wearer of the intricacy with which life is formed.

Swan The symbol of the swan is traditionally said to be a guide into dreamtime, giving access to hidden parts of us that are closed in the unconscious.

Sword The sword represents justice and authority. It is a powerful protection against all forms of harm and suggests courage and strength.

Tree This is a universal symbol depicting the interrelationship between the spiritual and physical.

Turtle Wear a gold turtle-shaped amulet for spiritual protection (particularly against psychic attack), stimulation of creativity, and enhanced fortune-telling powers.

Unicorn The unicorn is an ancient symbol of protection.

Wolf A potent and powerful animal, the wolf stands for Earth wisdom, knowledge, and protection.

Yin Yang Both an ancient and modern symbol, the yin yang is the embodiment and unification of all opposites.

Elemental Magic

FIRE, AIR, WATER, EARTH

In this type of magic, the elements of the Universe—Fire, Earth, Air, and Water—are called upon to give added power and extra energy to your spells!

Earth The direction of this element is North, and its hues are usually green. It is feminine and can be represented on an altar using crystals, salt, or sand. Its themes are recovery, healing, answers, knowledge, blessing, creating, and shielding.

> You may find that you work best with one of the elements. People drawn to candle magic, for example, are often drawn to working with Fire, while those who are drawn to incense are using both Air and Earth.

Air The direction for Air is East, and its hue is most often yellow. Incense represents Air on an altar, as the movement of the air can be seen in the smoke. Its themes are thinking, new ideas, finding inspiration, breaking free from the past or undesired situations, and physical movement.

Fire The direction of fire is South and is usually represented on an altar by a candle. Its hue is red, and it is associated with power, determination, and passionate energy. It is used for protection, cleansing, and creativity. It is associated with action or "doing."

Water Water is the element for the West and is represented by a bowl of water or other liquid, such as fruit juice. Its hue is usually blue, and it is associated with the sea, rain, snow, and rivers. Its themes are cleansing, revitalizing, removing unwanted spells, or changes of any kind. It is also associated with feeling.

The four elements are energies, and manifestations of energy, that make up the entire universe. Each element has its own power and is known for having certain qualities, natures, moods, and magical purposes.

THE FIFTH ELEMENT

The fifth element is that of Spirit. It is intangible yet that which makes everything happen. As a spell-caster, you are its representative and channel, so in using the other elements in magical working, you have a responsibility to act wisely and well.

An Incantation for the Four Elements

Drumming and chanting can help raise the vibration of this incantation.

METHOD:

- Simply speak the following words with passion:

SPIRIT OF FIRE,
SPIRIT OF EARTH,
SPIRIT OF AIR,
SPIRIT OF WATER:
JOIN WITH ME NOW!

- Now state the purpose of your spell!

To Summon Help from the Elements

This is another simple way of connecting to the power of the elements in preparation for spell-casting.

YOU WILL NEED:

- One white candle (Fire)
- A small bowl of salt or sand (Earth)
- A small bowl of water (Water)
- Bergamot incense (Air)
- A lighter

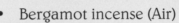

METHOD:

- Light the candle and incense.
- Call upon the power of Fire and Air, and ask them for their help in the work that you are about to do.
- Lift the bowl of salt to invoke the powers of Earth.
- Do the same with the water.
- When you have finished, pour the water onto the Earth, bury the ashes of the incense, and carefully snuff out the candle.

A Love Tree Spell

This spell uses all the elements in a very simple way. As with all love spells, always take responsibility for what you do.

YOU WILL NEED:

- 2 leaves on which you can draw
- Pencil or pen
- Green thread
- Needle and thread
- Seven pennies

METHOD:

- On one of the leaves, draw an image of yourself.
- On the other, draw a representation of your ideal love.
- Using the thread, sew the leaves together and knot the thread tightly.
- Find a tree you love; then hide the leaf inside a natural crevice or hole, securing it well. As you do this, say:

TREE OF EARTH, WATER, AIR, AND FIRE, GRANT ME THE LOVE THAT I DESIRE.

- Bury seven pennies at the base of the tree.
- Visit the tree regularly!

Making Charms

A Charming Technique

This chapter introduces you to some charms as magical objects. When you next give someone a present, consider "charming" the gift to enhance its power and make it even more significant.

YOU WILL NEED:

- A charm in the form of a heart (gold for male or silver for female)

METHOD:

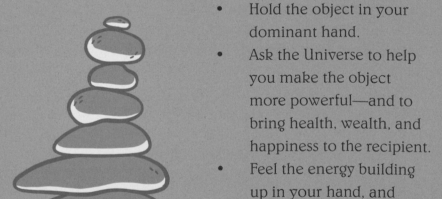

- Hold the object in your dominant hand.
- Ask the Universe to help you make the object more powerful—and to bring health, wealth, and happiness to the recipient.
- Feel the energy building up in your hand, and allow it to flow into the object.
- When you feel that the object is completely charged, "seal" it with the words:

HEALTH I BRING YOU, HAPPINESS TOO, WEALTH HEREIN, AND ALL FOR YOU.

Always cleanse your charm before it is given away. You can do this by leaving it in direct sunlight or by washing it in salt water.

Witch's Ladder Charms

This type of charm can be used in two different ways. It can be a general-purpose charm for protection and good luck, or it can be used for a particular intention.

A GENERAL-PURPOSE CHARM

This ladder should be made on the night of the Full Moon.

Red object for physical energy

Blue object for knowledge, peace, and protection

Yellow for happiness, prosperity, and emotional matters

Green for self-awareness and matters of health

Brown for steadiness and respect for others

Black for mystical insight and wisdom

Grey or white for spiritual harmony and balance

Feathers with markings (e.g., peacock feathers) for protection and clairvoyant abilities

YOU WILL NEED:

- White candles
- Incense (of your choice)
- Water
- White cord
- Red cord
- Black cord
- A lighter
- Objects from the ladder on the opposite page

METHOD:

- Gather your spell-making items; then light the candle and incense.
- Using about 1 m (3.3 ft) of each cord, tie the ends and braid them together while saying:

CORD OF RED,
CORD OF BLACK,
CORD OF WHITE,
WORK ENCHANTMENT HERE TONIGHT.

- About every 8 cm (3 in), securely knot in the objects. While doing this, set your intention. For example, for your yellow object, you could say:

WITH THIS [OBJECT NAME] AND THIS STRING, PROSPERITY THIS CHARM WILL BRING.

- Repeat until the braid is finished. Tie a knot at the end.
- Tie both ends of the braid together to form a circle.
- Pass the finished "ladder" above the candle flame (making sure it doesn't touch the flame). Then pass it through the incense smoke.
- Sprinkle the ladder with water, and say:

IN THE NAMES OF THE GOD AND THE GODDESS, BY AIR, EARTH, FIRE, AND WATER I DO THEE BLESS. OF OBJECTS NINE AND CORDS OF THREE, AS I WILL, SO SHALL IT BE.

- Hang the ladder where you'll see it daily, but where it doesn't get in the way.

A SPECIFIC-PURPOSE CHARM

The method for a specific-purpose charm is the same as for the general-purpose charm; however, you must make sure that your objects are geared toward your specific purpose!

You will usually only need three objects, which should make the charm a little easier to set up. The three items should represent the body, mind, and spirit.

MAKE A CHARM BAG

This bag is suitable for keeping your charms, crystals, amulets, and other magical objects safe. The bag can vary in size so adjust the measurements as you need to!

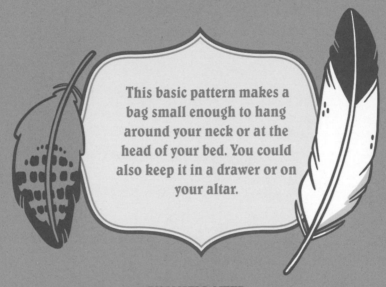

This basic pattern makes a bag small enough to hang around your neck or at the head of your bed. You could also keep it in a drawer or on your altar.

YOU WILL NEED:

- Your preferred material, at least 30 cm (4.5 in) square
- A length of cord around 1 m (3.3 ft) long
- An instrument such as an awl to make holes
- A circular template (about the size of a small plate)
- Your crystals, charms, etc.

METHOD:

- Cut out a circle from the material using the template.
- Make holes at regular intervals around the material approximately 2.5 cm (1 in) from the edge.
- Thread the cord through the holes, and pull it into a pouch shape.
- Think about the significance of the bag you are making—you are creating something that could change your life!
- Place your objects inside, and pull the cord tight.
- Wrap the cord around the top, and tie it securely.
- Sit quietly holding your bag. Think of all the symbolism and energies that you have put into it.

A Money Charm

Once you have made this charm, meditate daily on the money that you want. Be as realistic as possible, imagining the best way to use the cash!

YOU WILL NEED:

- A square of green cloth
- Allspice, borage, lavender, and saffron
- Rock salt
- Three silver coins
- Gold and silver thread

METHOD:

- Gather the three silver coins.
- Breathe on them four times and say:

TO THE SPIRITS OF THE AIR I SAY, BRING SOME MONEY MY WAY.

- Put the ingredients on the cloth.
- Tie the cloth into a bag.
- Fold the thread in two, and tie the knots around the neck of the bag. Use eight knots in the thread.
- Hide the bag in a safe, cool, dark place for eight days.
- After eight days, money should start coming in!

Herbal Charm to Attract Love

YOU WILL NEED:

- A circle of red cloth
- Any of the following: acacia, rose, myrtle, jasmine, or lavender petals
- A red felt heart
- Copper coin or ring
- Blue thread or ribbon

METHOD:

- As you fill the cloth with your items, imagine the kind of love interest you are looking for.
- Tie the cloth with blue thread or ribbon, in seven knots.
- As you tie the knots, chant an incantation such as:

SEVEN KNOWS I TIE ABOVE,
SEVEN KNOTS FOR ME AND LOVE.

- Hang it at the top of your bed, and await the results!

A Love Charm

This love charm calls for birch and is used to tell the Universe when you are ready to take on the responsibility of partnership.

YOU WILL NEED:

- Strips of birch bark gathered during the New Moon
- Red ink and pen
- Rose incense

METHOD:

- Write on the birch strip: "Bring me true love."
- Cast the bark into a stream and say,

MESSAGE OF LOVE, I SET YOU FREE, TO CAPTURE A LOVE AND RETURN TO ME.

A Charm Ball

This charm ball represents your new self with all its dreams and aspirations.

YOU WILL NEED:

- Hawthorn twigs
- White ribbon

METHOD:

- Weave together a ball from the twigs. As you do so, visualize what you hope for in the coming year.
- Tie a white ribbon around it— then hang it in a window or doorway.

Index

LOOK AT THIS LIFE—ALL MYSTERY AND MAGIC.

HARRY HOUDINI

Other titles in the series:
Spells * Crystals * Astrology * Palm Reading *
Divination * Manifesting * Tarot